Shattered And Mended By Christ

Kareen Robinson

Shattered And Mended By Christ

Publisher: Kareen Robinson

Book design: Williams DocuPrep
www.williamsdocuprep.com

Contents

Dedication

This book is dedicated to my
children, Andreen and Andre East,
my gifts, my blessings, my sunshine,
and my why.

Kareen Robinson

Mom

As a child, my life was good. There were happy memories, at least before my mother died. I was raised in a happy home with my extended family which included my father, brother, sister, aunt, and grandmother. My mom was terminally ill. She had Lupus and spent most of her time in the hospital. Before she was diagnosed, one of her kidneys had failed, and her body was poisoned.

My mom had a warm, caring, and loving personality. She was also very understanding. When she was feeling fairly good, she would be full of life. She always encouraged me and my brother to do our best at everything we did. She liked combing my hair, and when she did, she would tell me about her illness and how it affected her.

By the time I was seven years old, Mom began telling me that I was to take good care of my father and older brother. She also began to tell me that I would have a new mother and that I should treat my new mom just like my biological mother. I was young and did not understand much of this.

My family decided to celebrate my eighth birthday in style and held my first and only birthday party. My mom was not present. She was in the hospital—her home away from home. I did not miss her presence at all because I knew she could not make it, and my dad did an excellent job of keeping me entertained and happy, not just on my birthday but every day. I can safely say that I was Daddy's little girl, and he was my world.

Many pictures were taken and sent to my mother. She commented on the back of each one. Those pictures were placed in an album, which I cherish to this day. This is my only tangible memory of my mom. I saw Mom a few more times after my birthday in the form of house visits, which would last a few days, then off to the hospital once more.

The Most Difficult Day

My ninth birthday, June 5th, 1987, was a very traumatic and emotional day. My mother had come to visit, but she was having some complications and difficulty breathing. My dad went to borrow his friend's car to take her to the hospital. My brother and I were awakened to assist my grandmother and sister with my mom.

My mother, in her unstable state, called me to her and handed me my birthday gift that we had gone shopping for just days before. She whispered in my ear, "I love you," and reminded me to take care of my dad and my brother and to remember to give my brother Cary his birthday present that was hidden under her bed on his birthday. Cary's birthday is December 23rd, six months after mine. Then she hugged me, shouted, and slapped at me like never before. I was confused and hurt, so I went out into the yard to play with my brother.

My grandmother was getting my mom ready to go to the hospital when she suddenly screamed. My siblings and I ran to the bathroom to see our mother lying on the floor. We tried to see if my mom had just fainted, which was common for her, but there was no pulse. She was not breathing, and froth was running from her mouth. Dad had not returned yet, and I wondered what was keeping him. I questioned it, but nobody answered.

When my dad drove up in his friend's car, Grandma greeted him with the news. He jumped the gully in the front yard and ran to see for himself. After he was satisfied with his own checks, he retreated to his room and cried while looking through the window at the vehicle. I could see how deeply he was hurting. I did not want him to see me, so I sat on the other side of the wall below the window and cried. Making sure he didn't see me, I glanced up at him from time to time. This was the first time I saw my dad cry.

The police came to the house, and the necessary reports were made. The funeral home was contacted, and my mom's body was picked up. It was a Friday, but my brother and I didn't go to school. I have no more memories of this day after my mom's body was collected.

The days after were really challenging for my family. Funeral plans and family conflicts associated with the stress of my mom's passing were present. The funeral was extremely emotional. I remember bits of the church service, but what stood out most was the burial and lowering of the casket. I jumped in and held on to the casket for dear life. I did not want to see my mother's body lowered into the ground.

This was my first funeral. To this day, I don't like attending funerals. I only attend them in a few exceptional cases. People may view this as selfish and inconsiderate, but it isn't. I easily relate to those who have lost a loved one and give comfort when possible, but I find it difficult to appear at the church service and especially the burial. My grief has not ended, and I still relive moments of my mom's passing and funeral.

After the funeral, we tried to move on as a family, but things got more and more shaky, and the family suffered another loss in the form of separation. My grandmother, my sister, and my aunt, who I grew up with, left for reasons unknown to me.

Family life now had some additional stresses and responsibilities. My family had now become my dad, my brother, and me. There was no more grandma, who kept us all together and comforted me. Who made my favorite meals and treated my multiple wounds. I was an active child, so I got injured almost daily. No more auntie to tell funny stories and jokes. No big sister, though I was not fond of her, I liked having her around. No more aunties and cousins who would visit us regularly and were our play companions. The changes were made without explanation to me, as my family members moved, and I was forbidden to get in touch with them.

The changes were significant. With the new family dynamic came some additional stress as responsibilities increased. My dad, being the trooper he is, tried to incorporate some fun into our days, but the love, care, and sense of family were almost destroyed. No one spoke about how my mom's death and the family split affected us.

We tried to pick up the pieces and move on as if nothing had happened. We were hurting inside, but showing strength on the outside. For me, this strength came in the form of assisting my dad around the house. My neighbors were very helpful and supported us as best they could.

My mom was a teacher, and she placed much emphasis on a solid education. My dad was a policeman at the time, and there was no way my siblings and I could get away one day without doing homework. Our parents ensured that we did homework every day, even when we got none at school. However, due to the lack of grief counseling and in my own effort to forget my pain, I began to regress in school.

As things changed and I tried to adjust, it became evident to me that I was losing my ability to read. Every time I attempted to read, I began to cry. The words became blurry, and I couldn't tell what the word was. I cried because I knew the words but couldn't remember them.

My homework support base, which consisted of my grandma, mom, and dad, was gone. Well, my dad was physically there, but the pain and grief of losing my mother swallowed him up. He could no longer relate to me, and the fact that I looked so much like my mom reminded him daily of his loss, even though he made no mention of it.

Two years after my mom's death, my dad decided to remarry. With this marriage, he would provide us with a much needed mother figure and a loving companion for himself. However, this plan, even with the best of intentions, did not go smoothly.

My dad decided to continue and, of course, forget the past. This laid the foundation for years of family woes. I don't blame him for anything because I believe that he was trying his best to create a loving nuclear family. After thirty-plus years, the transition is still taking place.

My stepmother joined our family, and new relationships were formed. She was called 'mom' by me and my brother and was presented as our biological mother. This left me no room to mention my mom to anyone, especially to my dad. There was a huge difference between my stepmother's and my mom's personalities. My stepmother was young and inexperienced with children; she was unfriendly, rough, and forceful. All of which I think was to her disadvantage.

Life became increasingly confusing, and I did not take to the newness well. I rejected it, and outright refused to have my memories of my loving, caring, tender mom stripped from me.

Kareen Robinson

Identity Crisis

In high school, I began experiencing an identity crisis. I did not know who I was anymore. Everything in my life had turned upside down. The new family did not appeal to me. In addition to the reading battle I was having, there was now a sense of a lack of belonging. I felt strange in my own family—distant from everyone, misunderstood, and alone.

I became the source of many conflicts between my dad and stepmother. It was never my intention to be rude or hurt them, but often that was the result. My response was to do what was expected and stay out of trouble as best as possible. Yet I still found myself getting into problems daily. The real issue was not with me or my stepmother but with our differences in personalities.

Our personalities just did not mesh, and having to live with the concept of her being introduced as my biological mother really bothered me. It was devastating for me to get used to my dad giving her so much of the time we once shared. My dad was no longer mine.

It was often said that I was jealous of my stepmother. Honestly, I was not. I felt robbed. I had lost my mother, and now my dad. There was no longer a state of equilibrium. I lived in a house with many people but suffered silently. I loved my dad and cared for my stepmother, but I only existed among them. I smiled and hid my wounded heart. I spoke to very few people because I was seldom understood. I felt alienated and isolated.

School was no different. There were many challenges there, too. I daydreamed in class, played with the campus dogs, and had few friends and associates. At this point, I was repeating 10th Grade. I developed low self-esteem and low confidence. I was lonely, friendless, and had no sense of belonging. I didn't believe I deserved anything good in life and had no reason for living. I was a problem or source of pain for everyone, even myself.

I was practically emotionless. All I could feel was pain. Nothing mattered to me anymore and suicidal thoughts began to flood my mind. Happiness was a thing of the past. I would get glimpses of happiness while playing with my pet dogs or those on the school grounds. I was crushed and defeated, and to add insult to injury, in 11th Grade I was given a letter that said that due to poor academic performance I would not be a part of the Graduating Class of 1996. Here, I had lost it all.

I shared with my pastor that I had been struggling with thoughts of suicide the previous year and they were starting again. He soon introduced me to a friend of a life-time—not Christ, whom I had met before, but a friend in human form, Marley. Marley was always there to listen to me. We shared a few things in common: music, physical pain, and a deep love for our families. I was soon a member of his family. They loved me, cared for me, and supported and motivated me to carry on.

One day, on our way home, I told Marley that this was the end of it. I would find a way to end my life that evening. I told him that was nothing but a disappointment and failure to my family. It would be better for everyone if I just ended my life. I insisted he not follow me home as he normally did. I slowly walked home, taking a final look at everything and everyone.

When I got home, I placed a letter on my dad's bed explaining why I did what I did. I over medicated myself and went to the bathroom with a knife to slit my wrist. I did manage to cut my wrist, but not deep enough, and then the house phone rang. I thought it was my dad making his usual 4 p.m. call to see if I had made it home. Instead, it was Marley's mom telling me that he was on his way down to me and that she didn't want to lose her daughter. I cried because she took me as her own and thought I was valuable to her.

She continued to talk to me until Marley arrived, and then she hung up. Marley stayed with me until I fell asleep. As God would have it, I woke up the next morning and went through my everyday routine. My dad never mentioned anything about that letter. I am not even sure he saw it.

Marley and I studied together for the C.X.C. exam as often as possible to prove to my family and myself that I was not a total failure. Life at home with my family was not any better, but I now had another family with whom I was comfortable. At Marley's house, I could get away from the chaos in my life at home.

I didn't sleep well at night, mainly due to stress and a lack of comfort. Things were so calm at Marley's that I would fall asleep in Marley's bed each day after listening to his Boyz II Men album, among others. I would sleep for approximately two hours and run home before my dad got home from work.

The love I received from my pastor, second dad, Marley, and his entire family, along with my choir family and loving neighbors, helped bring me through those dark moments, but nothing surpassed the spiritual encounters and growth I experienced during this same period.

I give thanks to my Lord and Savior for each spiritual encounter along the way. For me, the choir was an outlet. I loved worshiping God through music. I plunged myself into each song. I began to love myself again and see the good in my life.

The C.X.C. results came out. I was elated that I passed most of my subjects. When I went into the school office to collect my results the teacher who handed it to me said, "Congratulations! Would you like to go on to the sixth grade?"

I said no and ran outside to my dad in his van. I gave him my results slip with a broad smile on my face. He opened it and said, "You would do better if you studied harder. You were a straight-A student before, and now it has come to this!"

I was a straight-A student prior to my mother's death, but ever since then I struggled and was a failing student, so now that I was on the rebound, I would not have him steal my joy. I was still happy within and made no mention of sixth grade. I had other plans.

The College Years

Marley and I applied to the community college to do a computer class full-time. I was enrolled in evening school to redo some math and English classes. Community college was very eye-opening for me. Academically, it was challenging, but it was my best year socially. I met a person of interest named Chad, and I became a part of a social group.

The joy, love, and happiness I experienced during my college years were beyond belief. My parents just couldn't comprehend it. Instead of embracing the positive changes in my life, they found ways to extinguish what they didn't understand. My friendship with Marley was under attack, and we were banned from seeing each other. My parents told me I was not to be seen with him. Even worse, my relationship with Chad was discovered. How dare I think it was acceptable to have a boyfriend!

Marley and I remained close, and I made other friends. I did not feel excluded for the first time in a decade. I could interact with my peers. During break, a group of us would walk to the mall, play games, eat lunch, and return to classes.

I felt free to express myself, and I was having fun. I learned that I was sociable and loveable and that I could share love with another person in an intimate way. Happiness returned to my life, and I met someone special to share this happiness with. I began to live, not just survive.

My friendship circle and newfound love were my escape. The year was hard on my health, though. I encountered health problems that affected my overall performance. I had a two-hour class in a trailer classroom that was very hot, then three hours in a freezing computer lab. My body did not manage the temperature changes well.

Every Wednesday, this would make me ill. My joints would crick and hurt, and Marley or one of my other friends would have to help me out of class to "thaw out," as we called it. I would sit out in the warmth of the sun to help regulate my temperature, then go back to class. I didn't understand it because I always wore layers of clothes to keep warm. The doctor's office was my regular place.

When the school year ended, Chad and I were still a couple. Marley had migrated to the United States, and my friends and I applied to university. However, my plans to further my education crumbled when my parents became aware of my relationship with Chad. They made the decision not to pay my tuition because they felt that I should not attend the same institution as my boyfriend.

I watched my friends move on, and I had no best friend to talk with. Here I was again, friendless and feeling unworthy of love. I wondered how my parents could crush my dreams of working in the hospitality industry and owning my own business. I was out of school except for evening classes. My spirit was crushed, and I sank into depression.

Once again, suicidal thoughts came rushing through like a hurricane. I was sick regularly, and I was emotionally distressed. On one of my doctor visits, my doctor asked me about my personal life, so I shared my brokenness with him and even my intentions to end my life.

He suggested that I should not take things so hard and that I should keep in touch with my friends. He also said that I should not be forced to end my relationship with Chad, and proposed that I maintain it. I thought, "This is where my happiness is certain", so I followed my doctor's advice. I now had a reason for living. I rebelled against my parent's intentions, followed my heart, and reclaimed my life.

I began to feel some sense of happiness, but by this time, I knew something was seriously wrong with me. I had grown up with severe mood swings, grief, and trauma. I had an inability to detect my own emotions, and I certainly couldn't describe them. All I could relate to were deep levels of brokenness and a bit of happiness. I survived it all only by the grace of God.

The following academic year, my dad presented me with an application for Teachers College. He said, "This would be the last time he would fund my education, so don't mess it up." I completed the application and turned it in. I was accepted, so my academic journey continued. Being able to pursue my dream of becoming a teacher was fulfilling. Chad and I were still going strong. We enjoyed each other's company and were supportive of each other's studies.

During my final year of college, I was faced with additional challenges at home and school. I had the responsibilities of maintaining the house, except earning an income to pay the bills and keeping up with assignments and choir practice, which was my resting place. I was in love, but I could not find the time or the energy to put into my relationship with Chad. I had to choose between love and my studies, so I made the most logical decision. I chose my studies.

Reluctantly, I abruptly broke things off with Chad. I tried my best to explain things, but he couldn't understand. The decision was by no means easy. Four wonderful years had to come to an abrupt end. I could hardly believe it myself. My decision broke both of our hearts.

For several days, I cried my heart out. To ease my pain, I ended all contact with Chad, and he threw himself into his newly developed fish farm to work his sorrows away. I hung on and pursued my studies with the sole intention of gaining my certification.

I gained another friend. This time it was Nicholas. He lived in my community and loved music and dancing. Our friendship was much like the one me and Marley shared. Nicholas was there when I needed a shoulder to lean on, and I returned the favor.

We both had stepmothers and both of us were both often misunderstood by our family members. We understood each other's pain, and we were a tower of strength for one another. He finished college and began working, which took up most of his time. I was alone and often empty inside, and thoughts of suicide began creeping in again.

By this time, my father had moved to the United States to live with my stepmother. I was responsible for the house, my elderly uncle, my older brother, and the four dogs that lived there. I was in my late 20s and still living the life my parents wanted me to live.

I was clinically depressed and took tranquilizers to sleep. Unhealthy thoughts ran through my mind constantly. On one of my regular doctor visits, my doctor said, "Why are you so stressed? Why do you carry the cares of the world on your shoulders? You're smart and young. Your health is fading. Change the pace of your life and live."

I asked, "What do you mean, Doctor?"

He explained, "I told you on previous occasions that the only way to reduce your worries is to have a family of your own to care for." I left the doctor's office and went home. I sat on the front steps pondering the doctor's advice. and decided I was going to live, even though suicidal thoughts had been rushing through my mind like a stampede.

Before long, I met the father of my two children. He told me he was married but separated and about to be divorced. We became friends, and one thing led to another. I soon found out I was pregnant with my first child. I gave birth to my daughter when I was 29 years old.

My father was not at all pleased. He wanted his baby girl to get married and then have children, and the idea of me being with a married man was totally unacceptable, but nothing he said mattered. I was wrestling with life or death. I chose life, and I was not going to regret it.

My relationship with my daughter's father put a strain on my relationship with my dad. Things escalated, tempers flared, and I left the family home to make a life with my own family. Yes, I was rebellious and a bit naive, but I knew I had to do something different, and this was it.

My baby's father and I lived together for five years and had a second child during our relationship. This relationship was by no means exempt from problems, as we both entered it with issues of our own. After six years, our relationship began to crumble. It went beyond rescue, and we split up. When my baby's father moved out of our rented home.

After a year of being on my own with two young children, I moved back to my parents' house. My brother and elder uncle resided there, and let's say there was no warm welcome on my arrival. I was under a lot of pressure. I was barely holding on, working a full-time job, going to school part-time, and being there for a six-year-old and a one-year-old. I felt like running away, and I prayed for a paid vacation. Lord knows, I needed one.

One weekend, Chad called and asked if I would go to the FIFA World Cup in Brazil with him. He said he had won an all-expenses-paid trip for two, but had no companion to go with.

I laughed and said, "You're joking, right?"

He said, "No, didn't you see me on television?"

I said, "No. Stop pulling my leg."

He said, "Do you have a valid passport and visa?

I said, "Yes. Give me a few days to think about it."

He drove to my house to visit me and requested my passport information. The next thing I knew, I was making plans for my children's father to keep them so I could go to Brazil. Chad took me to get my vaccine so I could travel, and off we went. I did get my paid vacation. I was with a true friend and an old firestick. We had a good time together. During the trip we were ex-boyfriend and girlfriend.

We met a Bahamian couple who became our friends. The wife looked at me and whispered in my ear, "He did not bring you here to remain an Ex. I hope you are aware of that."

I didn't respond, but I gave her a look like, *how do you know that?*

She said, "Give him a year, and you will find out."

I guess she knew what she was talking about because Chad and I decided to give our relationship a try. Once again, I was in a stable relationship, hoping to get married. Unfortunately, our plans for happily ever after did not come true.

As our relationship progressed, it became clear that there were some major differences in our concepts of relationship and marriage. Talks to clarify this were often seen as a bother or a means to initiate an argument. What was a genuine concern became a source of confrontation and pain.

I was in a relationship that brought a lot of hurt and pain. My heart was broken again. No matter how hard I tried to make things work. It became unbearable. The problem was often said to be me.

This led to additional health issues, which I didn't need. The emotional pain as well as the daily pressures of being a full-time worker, single mom, and caregiver of my elderly uncle, who was now experiencing Sundown Syndrome, compounded and resulted in a massive flare-up that lasted about 11 months.

I lost most of my cognitive functions and the ability to move. Photosensitivity, which I struggled with all my life, and joint pains were now my daily servings. Pain was the order of the day. I was unable to work most of the time, and that placed a mental strain on me. My children and faith in God were my best support.

My doctor said it was a classic Lupus flare-up and ran blood work to determine that. Like the tests from my childhood, the results were negative, except this time a high level of inflammation was detected. I was placed on medications that only made me feel worse, so I decided to wean myself off them and pray for God's healing. As usual, God showed up for me and guided me to a natural healing solution.

I battled for life each and every day while being strong enough not to show my pain to my children, whom I sent to school as often as I could. Some days they refused to leave, and other days I couldn't physically get myself up to send them off.

There were a few people who gave me much appreciated aid without hesitation. My taxi drivers and friends who were at my beck and call to get my children to and from school or me to the doctor's office, which I visited multiple times a week. My neighbor, and his construction workers looked out for me and provided an outlet of interaction that I needed. I can't forget my neighbor who chopped Soursop leaves to help my nerves, as we say locally when people shake uncontrollably.

I took it day by day and learned to trust and rely on God. Some days were better than others, but I saw positive changes. My body has undergone shock, heartache, and life trauma. Getting to a place where I could accept all this was difficult. Improvement came as I allowed myself to journey through my past and give myself the well-deserved time to grieve.

Through God's wisdom, I learned how to love and forgive myself and those who contributed to my situation. Whether they knowingly or unknowingly contributed, I forgive them. My health has improved, but not to what it was before. My children and I are continuing to learn how to cope with the changes and enjoy each other's company.